CHEATING SOULMATE

THE CONSIDERATE CHEAT

SOLOMON M. U

TABLE OF CONTENTS

INTRODUCTION

Being a cheat can be very hard to cope with, most people think all cheats enjoy playing their games and are having the fun of their lives in lala-land.

Contrary to this, some cheats do not really enjoy what they find themselves indulging in, they really want to change for the better and makes amends, this is because they feel they are in bondage not being free around the pretty or handsome one that brings the sun into their life.

They want to be free once more, but they find themselves in a very difficult situation, which was created by them subconsciously, or a situation that was created by their personality, selfishness, or probably other reasons might be the cause of their cheating attitude, this may sound and look stupid to others who are faithful, but mind you everyone mindset is different and we tend to behave, think and act differently.

This book will be explaining how a chronic cheat was able to carry on with his life in a positive direction, I will be using a true-life story as our illustrations on topics that will be discussed in this book.

By the time you are through with this book, you will understand that not everyone cheats for pleasure, and even if they were ignorant and eventually find themselves in the game, some really want to change for the better.

Click on **purchase now** to continue reading this amazing discovering, or read more on amazon kindle unlimited.

CHAPTER ONE

THE GENESIS

Everyone was created with a pure mindset, we all develop our personality right from our family, to peer group, and places we find ourselves. People are not born cheats, they develop this attitude as they grow up, like I earlier said this could be because of various reasons.

Someone that was once a saint could automatically change to be a cheat overnight if being cheated on by his or her lover that he or she gave their heart and totally dropped their guild no matter their personality traits.

However, money, falling short of love, lack of proper communication, could also be significant reasons why people indulge in the act of cheating.

However, no matter the reason, cheating is not the proper way to act when you really want to take the outdoors of any relationship, when you cheat, it means you are being selfish, wanting to eat you cake and have it.

It is only proper to walk away from any relationship that you know it is not working, even after trying your best through various means. Cheating is not, and is never a road you should walk down.

Some people cheat out of revenge, they were once the saint in their previous relationship but immediately they were cheated on, they try to pay the favor back and most times they become engorged in the whole game and the individual that was once cheated on is now the master of cheating, and even having a degree in the act of cheating.

Let me share a story with you, you will find it interesting to know that someone's personality could be influenced in a negative way so greatly, this may eventually make them more of a cheat than the individual that influenced them negatively towards the wrong direction.

A young man named John who was a lovely and caring individual, his personality was topnotch, everyone admired his style and the way he handles his business.

During his early high school days, he was not in a relationship, he fully focused on his academic works, this made him one of the best in his class, he relates with everyone in a mutual manner and most people appreciated the way he interacted with them.

Some months passed, John started finding himself with the mis-guided students in the class, he suddenly started gambling, he now came to class always behind the bells. However, this new change did not affect his academic grades negatively, he was still among the best in his class and people wanted to still associate with him because of his smartness and intelligence.

Boom, a female course mate called Sarah was always around his way, anywhere he goes, he finds her around, their chemistry started to click in together and John was starting to lost in for Sarah.

At first, he was a little shy to communicate his intentions and feelings to her, he started communicating his feeling through a different mean like caring.

However, Sarah understood the game he was playing, as a matter of fact she felt the same way for him, she was only trying to play a lady here, wanting him to approach her first John started helping Sarah with her assignments and lot of school works, Sarah also tried to reciprocate this gesture in her own way, she went out of her way to please him, at a time she played a scam on her mother and got some cash just to sort out John's school fees. This act made John go crazily in love with her,

Mind you, you don't have to always use the sentence "I love you" to most men when trying to communicate your love for them. You just need to act it, stop using the words, use actions in the place of words.

Shortly after this act of Sarah, John eventually communicated his feeling to her and she accepted without even allowing a second move down the clock.

Now get the view, at this point, both of them were in a relationship that looks perfect to them, they even go as far as going against family pride and family impediments, at a point John was restricted from visiting Sarah.

Amazing these two great partners always find a way to get to see themselves even after school how.

During the weekend or vacations, John will endeavor to always pay her visits, he will secretly come to her environ and wait until Sarah's mom goes out for duty, then he will spend the whole day there.

There was one funny day when Sarah's mom came back home before the usual hour, John was still in her place, Sarah had to hide him in a funny and crazy position.

There was a day he was arrested for breaking the restriction order, but he did not stop going there, even when he is not having enough cash for transportation, he will walk down miles just to spend time with her.

Sarah did same, she never acted less, she always reciprocated John's sacrifices and made him felt loved.

Soon, they became the talk of the class, thereafter the talk of the school, at one time they won the best relationship challenge that was conducted by their school representatives.

Sarah was an average grade student at the time they first met, suddenly her grade started going upwards, she was now challenging with the best in the class, this was a huge positive impact from John.

John was not the outgoing type, he was neither the total introvert that sit indoor all day, he was the type that knows how to balance work with play, everything was always on the equilibrium level. This made him influenced Sarah's academic grades positively, and from being an average grade student, she was competing with the best.

At this point, any lady coming around John knows they will be placed on the secondary, as everyone knew he treated Sarah as his priority, female knew he will not even think of a relationship or even a kiss with another lady. They were so jealous of the way he totally loved her without any crake.

It took some months before he got his first kiss from her, and subsequently they had sex in a very romantic way.

At this point no one was cheating, they were not even thinking about the act, they both hated cheats, they were the relationship chancellors among their peer group. The both of them were able to help so many of their peers with their relationship troubles.

Cheating was not in the picture and they were both living like they were created on the same day, "love birds" right?

Read on and discover how John's heart was later crushed, and this eventually led to the changing of his personality from being a loving and caring partner to a chronic cheat.

CHAPTER TWO

DISTANCE, RELATIONSHIP AND HEARTBREAK

Distance is one of the major cause of relationship breakdown, most of the time people tend to change their behaviors when they are not always around you.

This does not apply to every relationship because some people actually enjoy distance relationship, as far the communication is constant, they don't have any problem with you, they don't even think of cheating even when you are not present.

However, some people don't feel the same way when their partner is far off, the distance gets to their head and then their skin, then they start to feel the impact, they immediately look for another individual to fill in the gap.

Let take for instance your partner lives in the next street, suddenly you got a good paying job in another city and you had to move from your initial resident, mind you, at the time you were still living close to your lover you could just take steps out to his or her resident, or probably both of you take the morning jogging together, you were always doing great things together, because distance was never an issue, you didn't even imagine it to be an issue.

Both of you tend to talk to yourselves more, even without knowing it, you feel so close to the point that before taking a slight decision, you see yourself communicating your thoughts with your partner, it could even be subconsciously, even the craziest things that you could not pick up the phone to communicate for.

Boom, immediately you moved out of your previous location you find it not imperative to let your partner know some funny things about your day, you find it not important to make a communication out of those little things that you used to talk about, this attitude is always portrayed by strong introverts, they begin to keep little things to themselves since it is their nation to act this way.

Supposing their partner was still close to them, they would have been able to disclose somethings to them, things that they can't make a phone call over. The partner might even decode the unusual feeling and ask questions that might eventually lead to lot of talking and subsequently good understanding.

Let us continue with John and Sarah from where we stopped in the first chapter, you will understand how distance can lead to heart break, and eventually changing the personality of a loving individual into a chronic cheat. I will also show you how to handle distance relationship if you really want things to work out.

The final year came and John and Sarah sat for their last examination in high school, they both scaled through this chapter of their academic life in a sitting, they decided to sit for their entrance examination into college.

Sadly, only Sarah got the admission into a tertiary institution and John did not, meanwhile Sarah got a part-time admission, that will require her to go through a three years programme instead of the normal two years for the diploma.

At this point John was felling down, he had the kind of personality that dislike failure, he always loves to meet his goals, and whenever he doesn't, he goes really depress. However, he knew this was one part of his life he had to work on.

Now he had to deal with the fact of coping with distance that will be introduced in the relationship, Sarah on her own end was not too happy that John will be far off, but this is one step they both have to take for their future.

On a January before Sarah relocated, her mom fell ill and she eventually died, her dad had divorced her mom long before this, about ten years ago.

Her father never acted like a father to her after the sad encounter with her mom, so she had grown up without the touch of a father, she was left with her uncle and elder sister to take care of her, her bills and fees. John was there all along with her during her hard time, he was with her all through the hard time.

A month after her mother's death she had to resume her academics in a different city far away from her previous location where John also live, finally the distance is going to set in and the picture on the harsh realities was still in the shadows.

John had to pick a job to keep him busy and able to assist Sarah financially too, this is because he had to wait for another one year before he could sit for another entrance examination into a tertiary institution.

He had to travel with her to her new city to sort for accommodation for her, they got a nice apartment, where they could have some privacy since John was the shy type, he was very delighted with the location of the apartment since if offers them privacy and it was twenty minutes' walk to her college, has passed two nights there before returning to his city, because he had to resume his new appointment the next day, he eventually paid sixty percentage of the rent for her that year.

The first three months pasted, they were coping really good, John always visited her once a month and pass a night there, even her neighbors got to know him because of his frequent visits, they were also doing greatly with their constant communication each day.

Suddenly, after the first six months things started to go towards the negative direction, she now makes awful excuses for not taking her calls, she is either busy with assignments or she is in class, or she is in a busy and noisy market, unembellished it at the back of your heart that something always comes up.

Their communication level was going down the drain suddenly, it has reduced with about seventy percent and she is not even complaining.

Anytime John visited her and tried to have sex with her, she immedicably flays up, she doesn't even allow him to hold her all through the night as they normally do. Her excuse was that she feels it was wrong to continue having sex with John as she has a feeling that her late mom will be angry with her if she continued doing this when still single.

She even told John that she was ready to end the relationship with him if he continued troubling her with the demand for sex, that he should pick between her and sex. However, John gave it a thought and decided to stay with her even without having sex.

John began to feel stupid and cheated, how do they got to this point, he was doing and playing his part judiciously but this same gesture was not reciprocated, he started to pounder about the whole new development and was asking questions.

Whenever he visited, at this point, she will prefer he remains indoor, she don't want anyone to know he was around anytime he visited, she was always busy with her phone smiling, and forgetting the fact that John was around and she will only see him for just twenty-four hours in a month.

A year passed and they continued the relationship in this new awful manner. Later that year she had an unwanted pregnancy and John was not responsible because he has not had sex with her for over some months, she wanted to get rid of it without informing her uncle or sister about it, then she came up with a rape story.

However, this time she came to John's city after informing him about the rape story on the phone, John was so pissed off and disappointed, but he decided to help her to get the pregnancy out of the picture, this was a very difficult time for the both of them.

After the process she switched back to her loving self and the relationship got better, however, this lasted for about a month, and then a month after she has returned back to her city she switched back to her regular annoying self. John was still coping with all the dramas and was still playing his parts in all manner.

Later that year, it was time for John to sit for another entrance examination. He came this time not just for visiting but to sit for his examination the next day, on this night Sarah opened up to him telling him that she has moved on and has another person already, John was just wasting his time all along, she was never raped.

John felt dejected and totally depressed, he cried all night, and Sarah was not even moved she slept like a baby or like a drunk companion.

At about five in the morning, John made the awful decision to change his personality, he told himself that he will never be treated like trash again in his life.

The next morning, he went for his examination dejected and depressed, he eventually failed the examination and could not secure the admission for the second year. However, Sarah was not bothered as she was enjoying her new life and was moving to her second year in school.

HERE ARE SOME SIGNAL YOU SHOULD NOT LOOK OFF IF EVENTUALLY YOUR PARTNER SHOWS THEM

When the rate of communication reduces, have it in mind that something or someone else is taking the time.

When the they always give you excuse about finance, know that they are spending on someone or something.

When they suddenly change their sex appetite, know that they might be getting it from someone else.

When they tell you that you could and are free to have sex with whoever you feel like having sex with, know that they are trying to push you away.

When they hide their phone from you, or placed it on silence when they are around you, or always smile at their phone and not ready to share the reason for that smile with you, know that there is someone else.

HERE IS HOW TO BETTER YOUR RELATIONSHIP EVEN WITH DISTANCE

However, you might notice all the changes and you decide to make the relationship work, you should do the following;

Endeavor to discuss the ongoing issues with your partner, but you have to be very polite, try to pick the best time and manner to do this.

Try to communicate frequently with your partner no matter what it takes, communication is the life wire of any relationship and it is the key to a successful distanced relationship.

Try to create time to visit your partner, no matter how tight your schedules are, endeavor to do this as this will show to your partner that you still care about the relationship and want it to work out.

Try to enjoy the little time that you have to spend together, don't allow technology take all your time, this pretty or handsome is just here for a little while.

Show your partner you still love him or her, show them you are being sincere about this, talk to them about hiding their phones.

Always think and act positively.

CHAPTER THREE

THE NEGATIVE OUTCOME OF A TOXIC RELATIONSHIP

Toxic relationship can push a loving and great personality into cheating, he or she might be living a honest life with his or her partner, suddenly one of them cheated and the other individual automatically changes their personality.

Someone that was once loving and caring immediately becomes a chronic cheat, most time they might even end the toxic relationship and then begin to act strange from their normal personality.

Someone that was a saint suddenly becomes the master player, the hurt that they got from the toxic relationship automatically change everything about their sincerity, they are now using the same tactics that was used against them for others.

They might move on with their lives with another partner, but they will continue to play the new game they just discovered. In most cases they might be in more than one serious relationship.

They do this as backup, they use relationship one to backup relationship two and uses relationship two to backup relationship one. This might sound and look so childish but as you know, no two person feels or act in the same manner at a time.

This individual is surely still suffering from the hurt they got from the previous toxic relationship that crushed their positive thinking.

However, this new attitude gradually develops and metamorphoses in this individual's life, before they realized this awful way of behaving, it has already generated a lifestyle in them and it becomes part of them, even when they try to change, they will find it so difficult to do so.

Let us continue with the story of John and Sarah, I will use this to explain how a toxic relationship can change one's personality for the worst and also the best possible ways to handle this when you find yourself in this position.

Read along, you will get to know some hidden misconceptions about some people around you, who has been branded a total cheat, you will also understand how to handle them right.

John eventually got admission into a different college in another city, at this time Sarah was in her third year and has already moved on, but she was still dragging her past, she still calls John, and at times and acted like she was missing him, this is because she was having an awful time with any relationship, she find herself.

However, John had already zeroed his mind against Sarah or any other lady that crossed his path, this was because of the failed and toxic relationship he had with Sarah, he put all his heart and soul to this particular relationship but it couldn't work out, this broke him to the very bottom.

John resumes class and was always isolating himself from people, he has grown to not trusting people, mind you he was in his first year and Sarah was in her third, however, he got a full time admission that will require him to go through an academic process for two years for his diploma, unlike Sarah that has to go through three years because hers was a part time study.

He was very bright and intelligent, it looked like he has kept his intellectual level and intelligence from his high school days, immediately he was one of the best students in his class during course works, and he was gradually getting recognition from his classmates and lecturers, meanwhile he was still hurt from the toxic relationship he had with Sarah and was looking to create any means to pay her the favor back.

He made a very good friend in class called Stanley, Stanley understood John's actions and the way he acted, initially the friendship was being fueled by their desire to learn and become one of the best in the college history, this two peers could do their studying the whole weekend without stepping out, yeah you could refer to them as "bookworms", "introverts", or any self-abstaining word that comes to your imagination. They both visited themselves regularly and even spend the weekends in each other places.

John eventually made friends with Stanley's neighbors and was close to one of them called Blessings, at this point he began the genesis of his cheating career, knowing he doesn't feel anything intimate about Blessing but he still went on telling her he loves her just to get under her pants and use her to erase the memories of the heartbreak caused by Sarah.

He became a cheat unknowingly, as for Blessing she was enjoying her time with her new found lover and it never crossed her mind that John was not in love with her, he only enjoyed the sex and attention she gave him,

Blessing was now a frequent guest in his apartment, meanwhile they spend most of their time on the bed hanging and changing different styles that pleased them, Blessing on her own was enjoying her time without the knowledge of John's true intentions, she was loving the sexual life so much that she never demanded anything financially related from John, although, she was not the demanding type.

During his first examination a group of friends Stanley, Anna and Elizabeth discovered they could complement each other academically but was lacking in some of the most important causes, they decided to give John an invitation to be a member of their reading group.

John acknowledged the invitation because he was a fan of whoever love to develop their intellectual abilities. The group now read together in the college library, in quiet places and at the apartment of any of them qt night.

The first examination was dragging close and the preparations intensified, the group now spend most of their nights together reading at any of their places. However, Stanley was very close to anna and John was close to Elizabeth during the time they spent together.

John was getting too intimate with Elizabeth, even when she told him she was in a relationship with a guy that lives in another city, he still could not stop gazing at her anytime they both spend time together.

On the last night to their final paper for their first examination, reading classes for the night was schedule once more, and this time the class was going to be held in John's place, everyone was expected to meet there at eight pm that day, they planned to read all night before heading to the examination hall the next morning.

At five pm Stanley called John telling him he could not make it to the class because something important came up, John was somehow nervous that he will be spending the night reading with two pretty ladies alone, he wanted to call off the class but Anna pleaded that she needed the class to properly prepare for the French language examination the next day.

Being considerate, John had to go with the initial plan, at the moment, he was expecting two well shaped ladies at his apartment all night, one of which he was crushing on, and was looking for any great opportunity to go under her pants.

At about seven pm that evening Elizabeth showed up at John's place for the class, they had to wait for Anna for an hour hoping she shows up. However, at nine pm Anna was nowhere close to John's place, they were still optimistic that she will arrive for the class but had to stay their reading class while waiting for her.

It was already ten pm when Anna eventually called through to notify the pair that she will not be able to make the class, at this time, both of the pair already knew what could happen that night.

They both continued reading and trying to avoid the fact that they really wanted to throw the book under the table and get down, mind you John was still in a sexual entanglement with Blessing, in fact he just had sex with her a day before.

At about twelve am they both dropped their books and John was watching a funny skit with the aid of his phone, Elizabeth was suddenly interested in this smiles, at this time they were both laid on the bed, Elizabeth was lying at the right side of the bed, John had to take his right hand which was holding the phone around her. And touch lead to touches and they both started having a good time.

At this moment, John officially became a cheat, you could say the cheat that was once cheated on. Elizabeth also became a cheat because she was in a relationship with another who lived in another city.

John never told Elizabeth about Blessing that night, he only told her about the hurts he got from his relationship with Sarah, and Elizabeth complimented the story with a story of the issues she was having with her relationship.

They both went for their French language examination the next day and returned back to John's place where they continued having sex all through the day. The next day Elizabeth had to travel for the semester break, and John told him he was doing same, he eventually did not, he only waited for her to board the bus, after which he hurriedly returned to Blessing's place where he spent another two days having great sex.

At this point John has laid the foundation as a chronic cheat, he really wanted to end the relationship with Blessing because he was not comfortable being a cheat, but he was scared of the outcome with Elizabeth, he doesn't want to be the looser, he wanted a backup plan and Blessing was that plan.

Now when you find yourself in this situation, you have to sit down and think properly, then you have to make a choice.

It is better to stay out of any relationship when you feel hurt from your previous relationship, try to put yourself in the shoes of the individual you are cheating on.

You don't have to start playing games with the heart and feelings of others, try your best to make your pick, inform the individual that you are not so interested in, and endeavor to tell them the true state of the relationship.

You have to remember that the earlier you take your decision the better for all the parties, if you continue your game you will only build your cheating career that always end up in doom.

Love is a beautiful thing so when you find one don't joke with it.

CHAPTER FOUR

THE CONSIDERATE CHEAT

Cheats and consideration, are cheats considerate? Can you ever use the word "considerate" for a cheat? Well, cheats are not considerate but are selfish.

Some cheats always feel and say they are considerate, and compliment the story that it is because their nature finds it difficult to hurt another.

They will rather kept things away from the cheated one, and wait for them to end the relationship themselves, you will never hear anything like it is over from them, they will keep on dragging you from point A to point B, telling you stories upon stories.

However, you should have this at the back of your mind that no one can run more than their shadow, you can only walk within your shadow. Now, here is what they do that make them feels they are eventually feel that are being considerate.

They will never tell you it is over, this is because they don't want to make you sad, they can't handle seeing you sad because of what they have done, 'that is being considerate right?

Their attitude will automatically change negatively, as they will not be their normal selves anymore. This is because they just want to show you signs and they want you to willing leave them, they want you to break the relationship yourself, they don't want to be seen as the game ender here.

Excuses will start to come up, unending reasons for not acting the normal way will start to come up

Do you know why cheats gives you so much excuses, I bet you do, well if you don't know why, cheats comes up with a million excuses because they always lie, they use one lie to cover the other, and when you are almost discovering the covered secret they recover it with another malicious excuse.

At times they even forget their lies and start missing up stories, when you ask, they will try to get you confused with another generated lie.

They hide their phones, and deletes their conversation, according to them, they are trying to keep this away from you because they are protecting the relationship and also guiding your heart.

Don't get used to it, sort it out, get to know the bottom line of every new attitude your partner gives you.

Let continue with the story of John and use this to explain how a cheat always feel they are considerate.

John resumed the next academic section and decided to continue playing the double dating game with Blessing and Elizabeth according to him this was because during the previous holiday, anytime he called Elizabeth she was always with her other man in her city, they were always in a noisy party environ enjoying themselves, this made John felt he was just in a game.

However, Elizabeth promised him that she will stop seeing the guy and end everything to do with him, this was because she said her present partner was a cheat and also a hostile individual.

On resumption John will switch off his phone anytime he visited Blessing's and place his phone on silence anytime Elizabeth visited, he was feeling the heat of not being free at any point, but he placed the undisclosed secret at the top of everything.

According to him, he never wanted to hurt anyone, he rather carries the burden within himself, this act was killing him slowly, he was never free to express his love for Elizabeth.

On a good evening, Elizabeth felt the relationship ought to be taken to the next level, she called on John and told him she was ready to fully end everything to do with her other relationship only if John wanted it to be so, reluctantly, he accepted this offer knowing it is going to be more difficult coping with a very serious relationship and also having Blessing off the shore.

He went to see Blessing the next day, and was trying to look for a way to raise any form of argument with her, only for Blessing to be smarter than him, she always avoided anything that has to do with misunderstanding him.

John had no other choice than to continue his little paly game, he eventually got Blessing pregnant that same year, at this point, things was getting out of control.

Both parties agreed to take off the pregnancy, but John had to do this without the knowledge of Elizabeth. They eventually aborted the pregnancy, and Elizabeth got to know about the whole thing.

John thought he was playing a good game, but Elizabeth was one smart being, she somehow contacted Blessing and they both agreed to deal with John. They both decided to end the relationship with John.

Meanwhile Blessing gave John some money to keep for her, she immediately asked for her money, knowing John has spent the money, she also gave him a week to raise her money or she could take legal actions against him.

Elizabeth was very furious, she expected that John would have fully moved on with her after she left her previous relationship for him. However, she confronted him about the whole thing and told him to end the relationship with Blessing, if he was ready to soutinue a relationship with her.

John told her about the money issue he had with Blessing, and she agreed to help out, at this point John was fully convinced and decided he is going to move ahead in his life, he decided to end the relationship with Blessing the day he raised her money. Blessing was at first happy that everything has ended that way, but things changed when she got home.

As soon as Blessing got home, she started feeling the impact of heartbreak, she was so devastated with how her relationship with John eventually ended, she broke down emotionally and physically, she could not even have her meal, all she was thinking about was how to get back her man.

Her friends and roommate saw the way things was going, she was even anticipating suicide, they had to put a call across to John to let him know what the breakup have done to their friend.

When John heard the sad news he quickly rushed to Blessing's place, being considerate right? When he got there, he found himself caring for her because she was in a bad state because of his actions. He had to feed her, and eventually spent the night in her room.

At night she was feeling so cold and was even shaking after being covered with her sheet, John had to hold her tight that night, and eventually they had sex that night, and John had to promise her he will abandon his relationship with Elizabeth, he was simply doing this for her to get back to her feet once more.

At this point he was only fooling himself trying to please everyone, at first he made the right decision to abandon one relationship and focus on the other, but according to cheats association, he was being considerate.

At the end of the day he found himself entangled in the circle again. He decided to continue playing the smart game on both of them.

Now get this, as soon as you are having to pick from a list, you have to sit down and really think, then make your choice, and stand by it.

Try your best not to go back on your decision, try to express your desire to the party you don't want to continue a relationship with, at first, he or she might be really getting mad at you but it is better to go through this than to be a total cheat.

Learn to always control your feelings and stand by your choices when you make them, when you are positive and the next moment you are negative with your decision, you might be wanting too much as the best position to be is to be, is to take a stand whenever you make a decision.

On the other hand, when you are being cheated on and you miraculously found out, you should endeavor to discover if the cheat is ready to change, and when you discover that they are not ready to change for the better, it is better for you to run away without looking back.

Stop considering cheat when they don't need to be considered, you have to move on when you feel the time is right, as the outcome will be the best for you.

The only person you can't live without is yourself, get this at the back of your mind and stop saying or thinking that you can't live without your ex.

CHAPTER FIVE

THE TRAVELING CHEAT

Cheats and journeys are like five and six, most especially when they are cheating with another partner in a different city, at times they use their work requirement as excuses to travel out of the city.

Some persons that are experts in the game of cheating might even have their cheating partner in the same city with their "serious relationship".

They always give their partner a view that they are occupying a very important role in their organization, the impression will make you conclude that their organization can't even function without their presences, their names is always on the traveling list of the organization and are always with the boss.

At times this impression might be a fake setup, they only do this to create time for themselves, time they eventually spend with their cheating partners.

You will hear a statement like "honey I will be traveling with my boss next week and I think he has no one to stand in for me because he is always comfortable working with me".

However, if eventually your partner has cheated on you in the past and they are coming up with all sort of excuses, traveling excuses, bank issues and so on, you just have to look inward, something must be happening, something they are keeping away from you.

They will always tell you that they have financial challenges, this is because they are spending on another partner, trying to impress their cheating partner in crime, while you are struggling with them to get things better, this is the part that is really disgusting to watch or even imagine to do to anyone.

As a cheat you tend to spend more on things, most especially when you are a male cheat, you will automatically see your bills triple, this is because you will have to spend to keep things secret, you have to always make the calls at your continence time,

You just have to make that call when your partner is in the bath or just stepped out, because when you don't your cheating partner might call when you and your partner are watching a short funny skit on your phone, having to pick the call in their presences and trying to talk and act normal is one difficult thing to handle.

You will actually spend more on meals and other things when you are a cheat, if you were not cheating you would have not been thinking of paying for two, but as soon you start cheating you will have to pay more.

We will dive in more on the disadvantages and things you stand to lost when you are a chronic cheat.

Cheats love traveling so much, they love the word with passion even when their partner travels, they use the opportunity to fleet more in their absence, if they are the ones traveling, they use the opportunity to fleet as they feel so free from their partner.

Let us continue with our case study, our story with John and his found cheating attitude.

John and his friends had successfully rounded up their national diploma, they had to return to their home base John, Blessing and Elizabeth resided in different cities, this gave John the opportunity to be free to schedule his time to cheat with whoever he feels like doing it with.

He decided to pay his two partners visits on occasional bases. He travels to Elizabeth once in a month and do same to Blessing, he was practically spending all his income on keeping up with the both of them.

Whenever he visits Elizabeth, he acts like he has been missing her all this while, while whenever he visited Blessing, he acts like she was the only one in the picture.

Both ladies have fully gave their hearts to him, and he was finding it so difficult to break the bad news to any of them he doesn't want anymore.

Certainly, he found himself loving Elizabeth more than Blessing, this was because she understood him more than the other, however sex was also one of the major things which drive him out of control anytime he visited Elizabeth.

If you find yourself in the same situation as John, you really have to sit down and think about your future. Do you know that you are putting yourself through so much psychological trauma, aside yourself you are also wasting the future and the time of others that you are playing games with.

Endeavour to change your attitude, you could try visiting a chancellor, and when you eventually do you will have to open up to him or her totally, try not to keep them in the dark, they will certainly render help to you and try to draw you towards a positive direction.

If you find your partner acting in a different manner anytime they visit, you have to sit them down and ask questions, try to know the reason for the changes.

My dear, you have to think twice, you could give them the option of traveling with them to that meeting, no organization will resist you to spend the night with your love on in his room, so why not take that little vacation with them the next time they intend traveling.

Why not ask them that you feel like going through their phones in their presence when you feel they are hiding something.

However, you have to be really smart when you are doing this, technology has made it so easy to hide pictures and videos from you, they use these various advance applications to hide their files and picture they took with their cheating partner.

And the painful aspect is that, whenever they are visiting that other partner, they will hide yours and unhide those pictures they hide from you.

CHAPTER SIX

DISADVANTAGE OF BEING A CHEAT

As a cheat, there are various things you stand to lose. More often untrustworthiness is centered around the one being undermined, today, how about we take a gander at the negative impact it has on the person who swindles.

HERE ARE SOME THINGS CHEAT FIND THEMSELVES GOING THROUGH

It makes you a guarded

Out of nowhere, you feel everybody is out to get you. You turned out to be effectively bad-tempered out of dread you are going to get captured.

It makes you need harmony

You will change into a furious and anxious individual, wanting to make that call as soon as possible, because if you don't, she might walk in and catch you talking in a love tone to another lover.

It will open ways to additionally erring

Since you approve of cheating, continuously you'll approve of lying, being childish, offending in any event, being fierce.

It will destroy your relationship with God

You can't unhesitatingly move toward God realizing you are living in transgression.

Your character will be harmed

In one way or another, you won't be the decent individual you used to be. You will go to places that grasp your wrongdoing.

It will demolish your ethical compass

In one way or another, you won't have the guts to go to bat for what is correct. That will be tricky.

It will demolish your notoriety

In the long run, your issue will move into the open.

It may wreck your vocation

At the point when your notoriety is destroyed, you may pass up business bargains or even get terminated at work if the issue was with an individual partner.

It ruins your parenthood

Faithlessness discolors your heart yet youngsters react to virtue. You may battle confronting your kids. Kids get to the point of disloyalty, and your hands will be tired at that point.

Cheating distract your attention and it definitely eats a lot of your time

Abruptly you won't possess energy for what is significant in your life, Your family, your marriage, your vision, your support of the network.

It squanders your cash

A lot of your well-deserved cash you will toss at encounters and somebody that you cover up and won't last.

It segregates you

You will drive away from the individuals who might include an incentive in your life in light of the fact that. Undermining your accomplice doesn't just demolish your relationship yet it can likewise make irreversible harm the whole family. Infidelity was named as one of the greatest elements adding to most partitions.

Reasons were given by the individuals who cheat incorporate weariness, absence of enthusiastic help to downright old interest.

Anyway, for each activity, there's a response. For the normal man on the road, the aftermath of a deceiving embarrassment can some of the time be effectively contained anyway the equivalent can't be said for prominent characters.

In the event that you are thinking about wandering from your relationship think about these impediments first.

Notoriety

Those who regard you and hold you to an elevated expectation will be broken. What you have gone through years building could be crushed in a day.

Kids

Your kids are the honest casualties in this. Do they merit the embarrassment and disgrace a conning outrage could get them through?

Cash

Depending on whether you have a pre-matrimonial arrangement or not, your life partner could clear you out and leave you poor.

Sexually transmitted diseases and HIV, this needs no clarification.

So, before you go cheating and thinking of upgrading your status to a chronic cheat, you have to think through these demerits, why not just look the other way and make things right, your life will be far better if you can take this bold step.

Going back to John, after their graduation he spent eighty percent of his income keeping up with his cheat, everything went on the cost of various trips he made to these various cities to keep up with these relationships.

And this time, he was a low-income earner, now he spends on transportation, to these cities, aside this he also spends on hotel bills and also meals that are always on the high side in these hotels.

Save yourself from drowning, this water is getting so deep for you, you might not be lucky, if you cheat with someone that can't control their temper, they might even hurt you for real when they eventually find out.

John was not free even on social media, he could not post those lovely moment he had with this lady, because if he tried it the other will eventually get to see them and trouble will emanate from there.

I was once cheated on and I was once a cheat too, so when I pen down these statements you should be sure that you are hearing this from the horse's mount. It never paid me for one day, apart from the sex I ended up spending more than my capacity because I love pleasing my woman.

CHAPTER SEVEN

CHEATS ALWAYS COME BACK

There are barely anything that can harm your confidence more than discovering that an individual you adored, an individual you were in a serious relationship with, has undermined you.

It tosses your whole world into tumult. Since betrayal not just redirect you towards having sentiments it would make you think anything that comes your way is not genuine

Be that as it may, it additionally turns your mind against itself. It causes you to overlook that you're simply, and causes you to pose inquiries like, "would I say I was actually so repulsive that the individual needed to sneak around to discover any satisfaction throughout our time of dating?"

This self-question gets much additionally befuddling when the unavoidable happens the miscreant attempts to return to you.

It has neither rhyme nor reason. They went through days, months, here and there, a long time, sneaking around despite your good faith. Apparently, they weren't getting what they required from your relationship and they demonstrated that they didn't regard the relationship (or you) in the smallest manner.

You would believe that, in that circumstance, the individual who got discovered cheating would respect their extension back and keep things straight this time, but they will not change even after you accepted them back.

Get this at the back of your mind that con artists quite often return.

Everything originates from the way that your slippery little accomplice didn't have the fortitude to simply say, "Hello, I'm in a serious relationship.

Your miscreant needed everything both ways. They needed the adventure of the pursuit, the high of accomplishing something no-no, they needed mystery, freaky, secret sex and they yet still needed to return home to you around evening time.

Cheats decide to cheat as opposed to separation with you since they're designed to long for security as much as sex.

They're supporting their wagers. They don't confide in their little side piece, yet they do confide in you. They consider you to be a headquarters, as a steady, as something valid.

They need the security you furnish to exist next to each other with their mystery, childish "con artist" persona.

That is the reason when con artists are discovered, usually, they ask to remain.

In some cases, it's obvious. They argue, they guarantee, they state they've changed. And, at times, it's most certainly not. They text you unexpectedly, they sent you a Facebook message, they keep appearing at places you successive.

This makes you imagine that they need you back, however, don't get tricked.

They don't need you back. They need their familiar object back.

You gave them something to be thankful for. You enabled them to try, be a tease around, attempt things explicitly.

They realized they could confide in you, in spite of your issues. Perhaps you battled or they quit being pulled in to you. Or then again perhaps you were simply never that glad. You just clung to one another for comfort.

Be that as it may, whatever you had a sense of security to them. It was dependable. What's more, they're simply too chickenshit terrified to investigate their sexual alternatives again without having you secured as their wellbeing net. That is the reason they return.

It's not on the grounds that they understood what they have done. It's not on the grounds that they realize they committed the greatest error of their lives. It's not on the grounds that they love you.

This is on the grounds that you gave them a strong establishment to evaluate disloyalty and perceive how they loved it.

What's more, unfortunately, such a large number of them like it, and they need to discover their way back to that sweet set-up once more. Where they get somebody putting stock in them at home, while they attempt their karma with something new.

Try not to let yourself get bulldozed, at the point when they return, keep that entryway shut. Try not to permit yourself to be their anchor to the universe of decency.

Discover somebody who will love and trust you and who needs to test and investigate with you, and don't let anybody actually deal with you like you're insufficient for them.

Back to John.

John was trying to maintain his two relationships and doing his best to keep it away from colliding with each other, and then Blessing got to know about his fishing attitudes, she decided to end the relationship with John.

On the part of John, he never wanted to be seen as the cheat in the picture, he suddenly started changing his attitudes towards Blessing, acting up all the love game once more.

She suddenly fell in for the game not knowing she was only needed for the sex and distraction that she brought to John's life.

It was time for John and Elizabeth to sit for their entrance examination to higher national diploma. At this point Sarah was already undergoing hers, but she was also a part time student which she will be required to study for another three years, while John and Elizabeth applied for full time student that they will eventually complete in two years and graduate the same year as Sarah.

Remember chapter one, about John and Sarah the story is about to surface once more.

On the day of the examination, Sarah pleaded with John, that she will love to see him once more, John gave her a condition that they could only see in an open place which she agreed to.

After the examination both pairs met at the institution gate, Elizabeth was two poles away at that moment Sarah thought John was alone, she started to plead for his forgiveness, telling him to take her back.

Before she could finish her statement, Elizabeth showed up, then John introduced her in this manner, "Sarah meet my girl, the love of my life, Elizabeth meet Sarah my ex who I told you broke my heart".

Sarah was so outclassed by Elizabeth, she felt so inferior and knew at that moment that she was the one that lost the game.

John immediately told Sarah that they need to take their leave, she silently said goodbye. John knew he had won the game, he was so delighted in his spirit, he felt so gladden so much that he walked like a king.

Sarah further confirmed this feeling when she immediately sent John numerous messages pleading for him to take her back, at this moment she was ready to be the side chick.

They always come back, I give you my word on this, as soon as they see the gap that you filled in their lives, they immediately put a call across, they wouldn't mind traveling miles just to show you they still care.

They call friends close to you and convince them that they are a change personality, and they should help talk to you to have a change of mind and take them back.

Don't you ever make that mistake thinking they have changed and are ready to stick with you. This will only last for a while, they will eventually return to their way of life.

I tell you this, it is better to be broken once, than to be broken twice by the same individual.

CHAPTER EIGHT

HAVING A CHEAT AS YOUR SOULMATE

Having a cheat as a partner could be a very difficult road to go down, but having a chronic cheat as a soulmate is synonymous to living in hell with the devil himself.

How will you feel to be cheated on countless times and still remain in that so-called relationship, you should know that you are in a toxic relationship and flee before it gets to your head, and you start taking it as normalcy or it pushes you to act in an uncultured manner.

They treat you as trash, and run away from you in your hard time. You should have this in mind that leaving a toxic relationship is the best thing to do, it is never too late to make that move and find your right partner, don't let what you benefit from them make you stick with them.

Let continue with John.

John and Elizabeth eventually got admitted into the same institution as Sarah, it was the perfect environment for John to deal with Sarah, but much was waiting for him in the near future.

However, he was getting all the love from Elizabeth and he tend to love the game since Blessing was far off, he never allowed Blessing to visit him in school as he told her that they will never have privacy because he lied to her that he had a roommate which he didn't.

Elizabeth was eventually turning to be his soulmate, not knowing she was gradually getting into the clews of a chronic cheat.

Things was going well as John was trying to change from himself, they eventually stayed for a year without any major relationship issues, this was because John has gradually cut off his communications with Blessing. Until there final year when things went into lala-land.

John and Elizabeth were eventually roommate, they both decided to stay together to save funds, and John thought he could use the opportunity to change his attitude for the better since Elizabeth will always be around.

Everyone in their department knew them as a couple, and they were the envy of anyone in a relationship. But things change for the worst.

At a point, Elizabeth was not able to tolerate living with John because of his other crazy attitude, he was the king of introvert that would rather keep things to himself than share with anyone, aside that ladies was always wanting him because he was one of the best academically and facially in their department, he was also a senior member in the Student Union Governments.

All these made him a hot cake to have a piss for the ladies. Elizabeth was trying to cope with all this, but John was not helping the issue, he always gives these ladies the green light anytime they come his way.

It got to a month that John could not handle Elizabeth living with him anymore because both of them always engaged in physical combat, they sat down to discuss the predicament and they decided that Elizabeth will get another apartment close to John's place, so she could come over to his place anytime she wishes.

After the discussion, Elizabeth decided to pay a visit to her father in another city. John was so relived from living with her, he visited friends all though that weekend and did so much party.

On the day Elizabeth was to return, John got a call from a course mate called Millicent who was a easy one for all the guys in the department, she was calling for John to help him with her assignment and John could not go to her places, he asked her to come over to his place which she eventually did.

After the assignment, he decided to give her a walk, on their way he saw Elizabeth walking down towards them, he was immediately uncomfortable, because he knows she will think Millicent spent the weekend with him and he was only trying to send her off because he knows she will be returning that day. However, Millicent said hi to Elizabeth but she didn't respond,

John immediately turned back from that point and started walking home with Elizabeth, knowing he was in for a war with her.

On getting to the house she immediately asked for the fund John promised to give her for her apartment. John on his part not wanting any issues gave her his credit card to go get the money and both of them will go pay for the accommodation.

She was further furious thinking John was only trying to push her away from his life, she left the house in anger and went to withdraw all the money from John's account.

John was so furious but knew she will eventually come back home so he waited for her explanation, when she came, she started moving her things out, John looked at her and said "please you could have the money for your apartment, but please hand me over my balance that you withdrew from my account".

She didn't say a word, John quickly called in the oldest man in their apartment to wade into the matter, the man pleaded with Elizabeth for the money for about twenty minutes but she refused to return the money, she has gone to her friend's place and hide the money under her friend's bed without the friend knowing.

Thinks eventually escalated and went out of control, she got crazy and started throwing thing, she destroyed everything in the room, from the top to the bottom, according to her she started with him when he had nothing and she will destroy everything as she is about leaving.

She eventually got arrested and was locked up in police custody, at first on the first day she refused to give her statement so she was locked up for that night, the next morning she gave her statement and the police officers told her she has to return the cash and pay for the properties she destroyed.

She eventually returned the money but was unable to pay for the damage properties, John could not help seeing her suffer, he forfeited the properties and asked the police to let her go.

After her release she rented her apartment but could not stop asking for forgiveness from John, John being so embarrassed by the last occurrence accepted her but told her she could never visit him in his apartment anymore that he will be the only one visiting her.

She had no choice than to accept the bargain, but John used this opportunity to open a new chapter for cheating.

During the period Elizabeth was in police custody, John was being consoled by a new partner called Joy, this lady was trying to get into the picture and was using this opportunity to set in.

She asked John to spend the night in her place since his place was still under investigation, they eventually had sex and started a new game all through.

Even after John has accepted Elizabeth back, he was still having sex with Joy all along, until they graduated and moved to another city, he didn't stop until after a year of playing this game.

Now you have to listen to this, I am pleading with you don't let a toxic relationship push you to the wall, when you see you are not understanding the picture I think it is time for you to move out, you have to focus on your life first before any relationship.

Don't let that relationship push you to your low-low, just try your best to control yourself and move out of the relationship as quickly as possible.

You don't have to move in with your lover when you are not married, try to enjoy your singlehood, it is a lifetime that you will crave to have back when you get married.

CHAPTER NINE

WHEN A CHEAT LOVES

People thing that cheats never fall in love, but contrary to this they do, even when this hardly comes, but I tell you for sure, when anyone fall in love, they lose their brain a drop their guilds, cheats are no exception to this, even when theirs comes hardly.

When they see they can't live without you, they immediately start to advice themselves to change for the better, they begin to think of what to do and avoid hurting you, they also try to drop things that makes you feel bad, including cheating.

However, have it in mind that it is only a chronic cheat that can decide to stop their cheating attitude, you or a chancellor can only influence them towards this path.

When a cheat is in love, they could even go off guild to the point that they will give you the opportunity to visit them at any time, they might even give the option of moving in with them without paying bills.

They blow up with your thoughts, and always want to be around you, they are more clinching to their partners because they don't want anyone to be a barrier, they are always jealous lovers.

Let us go back to John.

After John moved to a different city, he met another lady named Sharon, both of them flowed quiet okay, but he was not able to forget Elizabeth.

He quickly travelled to her city and told her she could move in with him, in the city he lived, while she searches for a good job.

Elizabeth agreed to this opening and both of them lived together for about a year, during this period John was so faithful with his relationship, this was because he found out that no one could cope perfectly with him aside from his soulmate Elizabeth.

He treated her with a great level of respect and both individuals eventually got married a year later.

Everyone can change for the better only if they decide to do so, you as a person owe it to them to help influences this positive change.

But as much as you are trying to do this, don't forget your primary assignment, which is to first take care of yourself and your emotions intact, don't give room for your emotions to be toyed with.

Always know that before anything, your feeling, emotion and wellbeing should come first before any relationship.

I will love to get your feedback on the review and comment section, thank you for your time.